FAMILY BAND

MATTHEW GWATHMEY

Edited by Shane Neilson
Cover and book design by Jeremy Luke Hill
Proofread by Mary Hamilton
Set in Linux Libertine and fzm Embossed Label
Printed on Coach House Laid
Printed and bound by Arkay Design & Print

LIBRARY AND ARCHIVES CANADA CATALOGUING IN PUBLICATION

Title: Family band / Matthew Gwathmey.
Names: Gwathmey, Matthew, 1983- author.
Identifiers: Canadiana (print) 2024037066X | Canadiana (ebook) 20240370678 |
    ISBN 9781774221549 (softcover) | ISBN 9781774221563 (EPUB) |
    ISBN 9781774221556 (PDF)
Subjects: LCGFT: Poetry.
Classification: LCC PS8613.W38 F36 2024 | DDC C811/.6—dc23

The Porcupine's Quill gratefully acknowledges the support of the Canada Council for the Arts, the Ontario Arts Council, and the Ontario Book Publishing Tax Credit.

The Porcupine's Quill respectfully acknowledges the ancestral homelands of the Attawandaron, Anishinaabe, Haudenosaunee, and Métis Peoples, and recognizes that we are situated on Treaty 3 territory, the traditional territory of Mississaugas of the Credit First Nation.

The Porcupine's Quill also recognizes and supports the diverse persons who make up its community, regardless of race, age, culture, ability, ethnicity, nationality, gender identity and expression, sexual orientation, marital status, religious affiliation, and socioeconomic status.

The Porcupine's Quill
130 Dublin Street North
Guelph, Ontario, Canada
N1H 4N4
www.porcupinesquill.ca

For H.L. & J.G.

TABLE OF CONTENTS

ONE

TWO

THREE

FOUR

DAYSPRING PEDIGREE

More amorphous, speck-filled glow this morning.
Oozy, withered, alive again thankfully, the aloe vera houseplant.

Outside, in hawk and lark, the gathering soars.
Hellos pouring from our cousins embracing.

We, the visionaries turned huggers.
With an emotional attachment to rooster crows.

"I want a house thronging with abiotic perennials," says someone.
"I'm learning to play Brahms on the French horn," says another.

The all-pervading vinyl shower curtain bests me again.
Meanwhile talk about making hand and body soaps, donating used
    clothing.

Someone squeezes stacks of sent birthday cards, rickety and
    preposterous.
Another skims the AM radio acronyms and enthusiasts in their hopeful
    bubbles.

Our master plan—an empire of us.
Only enfolding afternoon ventures we have baby photos of.

Paper, tract of land, map, property pin, to hike!
I know I'll keep pulling at my beard until I remove that single white
    tusk.

Now "Nocturno: Woodwind Part" from up the lane.
Coffee plots tomorrow's plans at the absolute germinal zero-point
    dusk.

Spread of nighttime snacks (Chex Mix, chocolate vitamins) at first
    blush.
We grew our green thumbs during the recent dark-night-of-the-soul
    layover.

Use of a family reunion invite for a clasp and clutch.
Brings to the wee hours those who are welcome.

STARGAZING

At the time, we just had a refractor telescope near those woods studded
in cypress.

Pushing the finder to the North Star, all the while reading zodiacs.

First Taurus, his horns the size of skyscrapers, with Orion right beside.

Next a star near Neptune christened the fastest water-carrier in all five
lower heavens.

Pisces pulled us to the empyrean, not giving us pause for our usual
anecdotes.

Dragged to the bottom of Saturn, we continued gazing till there came a
ringing in our ears.

We figured we'd better come up for air, and above us swam Capricorn,
right on cue.

In a current of white dust appeared Libra's scales, our glass towards Venus.

Scorpio too busy practicing nebula spitting and galaxy strikes.

Then the reddish crab magnified its haze into our dials and family
eyepiece.

A backwards question mark, we called it Leo, that prickly flower of the
liminal frontier.

With our exact right hand, administering celestial sight by celestial sight.

No Virgo escaping us, though she sure made a valorous effort, nearly
vanishing in the cluster.

The moon by now a centaur eye bouncing around in our pocket.

When a ram came out from an opening, two orbs burned in a blanket.

Cloud cover moving in and nothing more to stare at except Gemini
doubled on top of airglow.

Clad in our jackets to shed the sudden storm, we dodged earthquakes
of new land stretching out.

And wouldn't you believe that in the meteor shower we lost the sky
charts.

Still though, not all of night swept to smash, fine as ground pepper.

Just heading home to drink some aqua fortis, sweetened with fire and
brimstone.

FAMILY BAND

What was there to do but to play music?
Me on guitar and my sister on fiddle.
Father came out after tuning to blow
the porch top off with his harmonica.
Then a second cousin, on seeing shingles
falling sure on embouchure, would bring
his five-string banjo, mumbling about picket
fences, Double Dutch and potluck suppers.

Singers, we always had lots of singers.
Back in the house, next door, up in the hollow.
Singers we couldn't hear. Singers we didn't want to.
Our songs turned out grief lessons:
"The Little Lost Child," "O Molly My Dear,"
"How Can We Stand Such Sorrow," "Bury Me
Under The Willow Weeping."

Nothing in return but quick toe taps
and off-beat claps, next tune chosen
by the fastest caller. That is,
until a few of our aunts came,
right hands flicking with rulers,
and made us all sing gospel hymns,
about life after life after.

                          when we frameshift before daybreak.
Then as we replicate our threadbare traits, we spawn back,
cloning them for the prenatal season soon to begin.
Eukaryote, an expanse fit for allele evolution,
its rolling bacteria and level archaea.
RNA now a zygote, a founder of progeny.
How did we reproduce? Struck haploid, fused our saint of gametes.
Two more conjugations, pressed against the fallopian.
We live quadrupled, our offspring cells and us, out along genome.
Polypeptide chains proclaim the carrying on of amino acids,
patron of triplet codes, promoter of germ layers.
Somehow the codon still fit, missense long faded,
the luster anomaly nearly forgotten.

IT SEEMED THAT WE HAD HARDLY
BEGUN AND WE WERE ALREADY THERE

There was work   loose folds of laundry   setting the forks
on the left   spoons on the right   cleaning toilets and sinks
every other weekend   that endless   battle with dust

perhaps we'll write down   some advice to pass on
perhaps we'll come up with   some new Greek myths

watching the same   movie again   we would recite   the
lines together   sing the soundtrack   do the actions   find
our names   in the credits

French toast breakfast   and dinner   pools of maple syrup
to lap up   cream if the season   a freezer full   of popsicles
the dessert cure-all

and broken pieces   of crayons   saved for a craft   we'll
never make

you don't have to tell me   whenever you go   to the
washroom   or take a drink   of water

he tried to curl   into you   sharing his   leg-kicking half-
sleep   demoting you   to the wool rug

then that time   we nearly lost one   in a snowbank   the
passing plow   and caving in   shouts to dig   for a gloved
hand   a reflective forearm

I've got to find out   who or what is   making that noise

child-proof the home   move everything up   three feet then
five   but where did   the glitter come from   and those
fingerprints   along the tops   of the windows

copying me   brushing teeth   incisors   canines molars   left
right front   top bottom side   tongue roof gums   attempts at
spitting

red rover red rover   send vaccines on over   starve a fever
feed a cold   temperatures took   for that magic number
one-o-four   when we'd need   a midnight trip

to find the baby   follow the trail   of kitchenwares

fake snoring   to stay up longer   a treasury   of folktales
try counting sheep   try the number   of glow-up stars

moods flared   and erupted   a separate couch   for everyone

boxes of hand-me-downs   labelled in black marker   beside
the containers   of mittens for winter   sandals for summer
the effort we spent   moving our belongings   from one
place   to another

then that time   we took the trip   until it became   just a
hunch or inkling   of something   extraordinary   after all
the souvenirs eaten   the cheese the pesto   the olive oil
galore   or diminished   to trinkets to knick-knacks

our house turning   into a leaky ship   for the April thaw

the questions came   do you die   after your party   when
you turn a hundred   what kind of person   eats blue cheese
where does your sense   of touch go   in a blizzard   any
difference   between whistle and hum

camped out laying   at either end   of the mattress   in the
six-person tent   stuffed animals   covering the floor
marvels from   an earlier safari

and lunch   the scrounger's meal   here a carton   of
strawberries   sure eat the stems   here a tub   of yogurt
sure maybe outdated   or we'd push vegetables   peeled cut
and arranged   circling a bowl of dressing

we were always   levelling pictures   on the walls

the shower the only   hiding place   as long as you
remembered   to lock the door   and remove all hairpins

there was playing   favourite sport   changed daily   two
packs of face cards   one for the carpet   one for the table
the refashioning   of sticks and rocks   the toys that   no
longer fit   in their boxes

perhaps we'll dig up   the dandelions   perhaps we'll read
up   on the epistles

but we had   the photos of course   and maybe   even better
working with   real prints again   the easy slide   into each
clear sleeve

then that time   the bird fell from the sky   a few feet from
one of them   we all gathered   around it   the sliced neck
the dark brown feathers   and all I could   think to say   that
kids is death   get a plastic bag   let's clean it up.

You chase | aches, a dozen | zoned oceans | canoes, oceanic |
cocaine unseals | sensual, wreathes | weathers. Sister | resist.
The night | thing in dusty | study. Part | trap, trashed | hardest, the
unbred | burden cried | cider. Silent | listen. The toneless | noteless
gods | dogs felt | left. Your keen | knee to spinal | plains, to hustling |
sunlight. At wand | dawn.

I swig | wigs, a restful | fluster. I failed | afield, so sink | skin down
slime | miles in sober | robes. The nicest | insect infests | fitness
lessons | sonless, my seaside | disease. Proton | pronto. Gaps | gasp
a friend | finder. Namely | laymen.

You praised | despair, relayed | layered antlers | rentals, plates |
petals from | form. Whoever lashes | hassle or lives | veils, bets |
best. Any | nay, the roasting | organist you saw | was needless |
lessened by a mono | moon.

I, a remote | meteor, a tame | team. My nudity | untidy. My elbow |
below the nude | dune. I lied | idle. Rustic | citrus filets | itself. I eat
| ate safest | feasts in a tacit | attic.

You, a saltier | realist, the last | salt. Your rescued | seducer, rescue
secure. Sit | 'tis an urn | run. Leg | gel has | ash. A looped | poodle
could | cloud your sector | escort. Ultimate | mutilate that evil | vile
viral | rival.

I, saint | stain. I begin | being a cellar | caller. Add | dad. Reset |
trees that react | trace forth | froth. Who | how when | hewn the pale
| plea? The nameless | salesman?

You, sleuth | hustle. Halls | shall sweat | waste, though exits | exist.
No | on laps | slap all loin | lion. The flesh | shelf per | rep. You surf
| furs both cool | loco, taste | state manors | ransom. South | shout
ah | ha, treason | senator!

I sample | maples, no save | vase. The noon | neon by kale | lake. I
turn | runt, the rifle | flier quite | quiet. The drier | rider, a sunlit |
insult. The surge | urges our relay | early. The grease | agrees, a
siren | rinse. Hearty | earthy, a tablet | battle now | won. A large |
glare. Ours | sour. My chit | itch, your west | stew, my freak | faker,
your late | tale.

You hated | death.

I stressed | desserts.

FACTS

Vegetables don't exist.
Fingernails grow from base to tip.
Cheetahs feint midair when chasing prey.
UFOs appear when Venus looms like a flagship.

If you travel the speed of light, you'll never age.
If you jump off a bridge, you turn to confetti.
If you run in the rain, you get fifty percent wetter.
If you fall in a black hole, you stretch out like spaghetti.

Some skunks smell each other from miles away.
Some bumblebee queens quack.
Some cars run on used French fry oil.
Some ants explode when attacked.

While helping you into your snow pants,
these are the facts I tell you.
In the garage, swing your partner round
and round—our quadrille square dance.

A baptism brought the family together.
(Baptists bought the pageantry tether.)
The eleventh commandment in mid-speech.
(The eleven commanded to pickle the peaches.)
Rosemount raised to glory amid the host of hosts.
(Roses mounted Glorias from the run-amok ghosts.)
That house, the crux of our brood in Sunday best.
(Household in flux, the bread our bread, decorum est.)
We gathered round the cross-shaped cherrystone.
(We blathered about our moss-covered backbones.)
Ate the full menu of serve-yourself casseroles.
(Ate the menu full, right down to the buttonhole.)
Traced each other with wax paper and chalk.
(Chased one another out among the cornstalks.)

HIDE & SEEK

You're at the nascondino championship & hide & seek calls its numbers to sixty & hide & seek sacrifices an abandoned ghost town known as the Land of Toys & hide & seek descends with a shout of "ready or not, here I come" & hide & seek spreads all the way out & hide & seek requires the skills of running, tracking, concealing, observing, staying silent & hide & seek promises we can vanquish death & hide & seek delivers messages of pure giveness, prophets dispensed without a care & hide & seek overtakes sardines in a tin can & hide & seek compiles park rules & hide & seek pelts down new manna & hide & seek questions a just city-state run by a just person & hide & seek resurrects the Christ-event in the second coming & hide & seek provides an exchange of gifts & hide & seek redirects talk of double agents & hide & seek revamps our childhood sanctum & hide & seek offers a large mattress that you can launch yourself towards & hide & seek reminds us that in Ohio, you must yell "free" when you reach home base & hide & seek dismisses merits, sins, irreparable parables & hide & seek bestows the impossible offering & hide & seek wakes the early bird & hide & seek misses the cache-cache & hide & seek values that stashed mole between the shoulder blades & hide & seek offers free Pauline relationship advice & hide & seek designates who's the seeker, blue shoe, blue shoe, who's it, not you & hide & seek ruptures coherence & hide & seek fires most sycophants & hide & seek flips the switch on philosophy's failure & hide & seek decides when you come out & hide & seek sprees in the joyous blessing of endless bounty & hide & seek pays your tag collectors, a thorn in our common side & hide & seek cast spells, apostleship, in view of a transformed world & hide & seek emanates olly olly oxen free & hide & seek plays only after dusk & hide & seek randomizes chance & hide & seek awards the golden fig leaf & hide & seek salutes a falling away & hide & seek delights touch-free & hide & seek surges benefits at the communion feast & hide & seek says tear down our monuments, I say, tear down & hide & seek catches us up together in the clouds & hide & seek promises we shall be changed for the better.

A RECIPE FOR RABIES

Take ragwort and chop it like your neighbour's butcher.
One thing to remember—you can't have too much *sucre*.
Other plants include spoonfuls of yarrow and wild sage,
the *feuilles* of white lilies, thistle dried in nightshade.
Take all and grind them into a coarse powder.
Add a walnut shell of *vin* or more for fear of water.
Rub it on the bite *depuis* mingled herbs turn pink,
to keep the sore from rankling, to keep you from doublethink.
Of course you have the euphoric nutmeg round your neck.
Of course you've kissed burdock root mixed with triple sec.
Still can't sleep? *Fermeture de ta gorge?* Eyes running wild?
Take a bath in the river, a swim to Emerald Isle.
If the pain still spreads, cutting through deep crevasse,
strap on salted potatoes cooked on a *fête de grâces*.

RE -

We rewired our wires. / We revamped our vampires.
We retraced our steps. / We rebuilt our palaces.
We repaid our loans. / We returned our thanks.
We rearranged our furniture. / We remodelled our home.
We reactivated our subscriptions. / We reversed our falls.
We reassessed our priorities. / We readjusted our concerns.
We reabsorbed our fluids. / We redrew our maps.
We rebooted our TV series. / We recapped our highlights.
We rebuffed our naysayers. / We rebuked our critics.
We recited our mantras. / We recycled our recyclables.
We released our hounds. / We recalled our calls.
We related our troubles. / We repaired our sinks.
We renewed our vows. / We relaxed our mores.
We removed our warts. / We reformatted our hard drives.
We reviewed our margin notes. / We referenced our inside jokes.
We repeated our mistakes. / We requested our friendships.
We rerouted our routers. / We revered our gods.
We refreshed our pages. / We reissued our issues.
We revisited our hotspots. / We reaffirmed our convictions.
We revised our documents. / We redeemed our coupons.
We rehearsed our lines. / We reinvented ourselves.
We researched our choices. / We renewed our membership.
We restarted our puzzle. / We retrieved our sticks.
We recharged our batteries. / We re-elected our officials.
We reframed our arguments. / We remedied our illness.
We repainted our fence. / We reinforced our walls.
We reposted our moments. / We recaptured our spark.
We refocused our attention. / We rehashed our chats.
We rewalked our walks. / We retalked our talks.
We revitalized our neighbourhood. / We reconstructed our past.

WHAT IT MEANT TO US
(A PARTIAL LIST)

For Mark

It meant goals formed by committee and logical conundrums.
It meant we weren't wise enough to play fools. To shake up social
    order. To respond to vice.
It meant expectant A-frame ganders with a host eager to dispense
    wafers.
It meant a growth the size of an orange.
It meant slicked hair, dressed in starch. A bit of nonsense in the spirit
    land of carnival. Marrying an uncomfortable resonance to our
    suspended hours.
It meant dipped in the basin. Crafty in our letters, using guile,
    eloquence and multiple personas.
It meant a prescription of daily bike rides.
It meant riffing on our house with the narrow gate and screened-in
    porch.
It meant drops of cloth squeezed out.
It meant possible. Rather than certain.
It meant a chanting pitch. A core insight.
It meant to garden the tubers and root veg in Eden.
It meant we operated on a different calendar, one measured by training,
    rest and marathons.
It meant never straightforward, but interwoven. Threads well-chosen.
It meant we held fast to particulars, the trail of inheritance.
It meant new languages invented. Dissident musings. Deliberate
    jesting. Dialogic standpoints.
It meant purblindness. Pure blindness. Robust repartee.
It meant all those hands.
It meant we tried every stalling tactic. Trial episodes. Targeted
    therapy. Miracle drugs. We lived as if the law meant nothing. We
    entertained a humble awareness of folly. Of plenitude.
    A bodily want for nothing.
It meant somehow the tumor's back.

Giving wind a name
makes it human.
When Hurricane Ian
and Hurricane
Josephine merge,
we dub the marriage
Josephian.
As a bloated river
hits a full-moon tide,
new islands rewrite
themselves in strands and inlets.
A levelling takes place,
reducing our monuments
to zero-sum.
Flowing, the role of thieving,
extending the Seven Seas,
sailing them.
The commander of squalls
catches the peak gust
revitalizing entire blocks.
While a white horse bolsters
curbside bins at a matinee.
The magnificence of worms,
they readily accept
any lending,
stage their own endgame.
At the outskirts
rests conjecture,
the outer banks
a rule of thumb.
Timeline's fuzzy here.
Three chasing arrows, yes,
but who creates the catchphrase?
Born out of canny thrift,
a confluence,
a great flood of loops,
teeming with cosmic optimists.

Tower cranes come
with aid, I think.
Then mobs in boats
to loot copper
telephone wires.
Elsewhere overbrims.
Loose power lines
hum urgent anthems.
Ye who are weary,
come bandwagon.
Stockpiles of debris,
the material heap,
stacked in the manner
of Lincoln Log cabins.
Taps spouting forth
about renewal,
salvaging e-waste.
Leftover crabs
in kitchen cabinets
pinch plastic pellets
and synthetic fabrics.
Do you remember the knots
we learned in scouts?
How about another round
for a couple hours
with your prom-queen crown?
Hometown contextual.
A migratory pattern.
Cyclical. Conceptual.

MONKVILLE

Providence   played a part   in our penance
of silence   and sack-wearing   and hair-growing.
Our ids brought   shipwreck experiences,
counterpoints of desire,   death to borrowed selves.
So we walk   the same   catholicon halo
with our Desert Fathers   in portentous discourse.
Of the eponymous constants,   Bohr's radius vital—
most probable distance   between the nucleus
and the electron   in a hydrogen atom.
Let the reneging   of campaign promises   begin.
No surgeons for tonsure.   No lay brothers for Latin.
Let us upgrade   our celibate   bed trick
for the eloping sons   and would-be fathers,
nullify the law   for some marvel hoards.
A delicate balance,   the monastic trifecta.
The trusty abbot,   our supposed advisor,
says to labour   with the all-important   scrub cloth.
Querying   the pan,   iron and present,
"will you cast   your black residue   in flecks or daubs?"
We consider lamina.   Consider veneer.
Meditate on through   limescale deposits.
Messianic time   contracted,   compressed.
You may ask—   "why do we garden thus?"
For hushed   martyrdom   in the trapeza.
Religious habit.   For cenobium,
community   shoulder to shoulder,   shoe to shoe,
the whole of our ensemble.   Come what will.
Come what may.   We live a little   every day.

COINCIDENTAL

A decade later, they did return.
Not much had changed.
Still room enough to make the dirt rise up.
To make the sky close its dark curtain
with their dance of harrow, plant, rake.
Ordinary folk of the world—
show your faces!
Proclaim yourselves fans of many of the same bands!
The deck loose and slack and propped up by one pole.
Turned up on the front step,
they just knocked and the door opened.
Their B-side demo track played "Back To The Old House."
As good a testament as any.
Carving the family name and their year there—
The Smiths, 1984.

Leaving the main river to fish the tributaries,
they traipsed in waders through mouths of brooks
and underwater springs, casting like *la plus légère,*
while their lines glanced at the surface,
a flicked wrist vulnerable to the marigold.
Déjeuner—barbecued in coals until the skin curled,
eaten with bread while the carcass went to nearby gulls.
Some tackle they upgraded *à cause de* passing fads,
some parts stayed with them—an old Pfleuger reel,
its quiet *pirouette* and click-pawl *chanson.*
They preferred to tie the Scottish fly patterns,
black body splitting to a lone hook and *queue.*
La lutte the brilliant same, dredging up
rolling knots they didn't teach anymore,
imaginary names for the shore's features.
They led the played fish over a scoop net *tête*-first
into the hoop, then hoisted their catch above,
flipping the evening's foam that had started to bubble up,
the required photo op and an empty bucket
of *vers libre* in the background.

                              on your head.
Walking on the mossy side of the ridge
sculpted by tree roots along the floor.

Over yonder, chiffon silk
fused with raw merino wool
reveals the felt universe.
Leaves model a bark pattern.

On the other side, resting upon layers
of up-cycle material,
a pine cone—each scale wired
to open and to close
with the fashion of the seasons.

Just in view, a single birch sapling,
fabric massaged in,
pretends for the canopy.

Further along, braided horsehair
bound to stem, looped on, stitched down,
an overflowing fruit fall,
investigating dead matter,
the certainty of solid ground.

Who else has stepped foot on this place?
Right here, by grosgrain lip,
worn path tilted up ahead,
elastic strap a trail that brings you
right back to the understory.

In itself significant. Throughout the forest, chestnuts or
hickories or northern reds. This time an antecedent.
Hugging a byway cut through. One splashed across.
Bringing up the uncertainty of scale, the embodied
presence of chance, corporeal finitude, ruddy aurora.
Zoomed out from our scene, the camera. Woods seemed
in penance. Say it: hit by a falling tree while driving
her car home from church. Trimming the trunk too thin,
elegant tools a strange role, pieces glued together in form.
Then a chair. Reciprocal. A space carved out for muffled
chit-chat. Others tried to sit, but found its dark-grained
angles inaccurate. With the first roll forward, the seat
spilled you out. Hours struggling there. Still others
encouraged us to make another. A memory palace of
rockers. To sing praises, not dirges. Uplifting alchemy,
the emphasis on gold and elixir encircling her. Say it:
she baked Alaska for our birthdays, ice cream and cake
topped with browned meringue, served after the largest
vegetables you've ever seen, record-setting cole crops.
As the touch of wood burned and cooled and called to mind.

Measuring the hide for choice of posture—straight upright,
right turn upright, left turn semi-sneak. The hunt on display.
Skinning off further fur to cover form, as much of the eyelids
as possible. Fleshing out the skull for any more chunks
of remaining tissue. Preserving the cape, a parallel to accept.
Never many new principles to discover in modelling clay.
A neon palm tree grows beside the shed's oak planks.
Anchoring stitches now. Crossed and subverted reversals.
Shattered and transformed pedestals. Preparing the mannequin.
Holes drilled to attach the bifurcated antlers to wood backing
with drywall screws. Losing a familiar sense of construct.
Dizzying ellipses of epoxy and baseball stitching hold
down areas that want to sag. Tucking in gathered skin.
Blending labels. Collapsing handles. Towser, Snap,
Quicksight, Racer, Babbler, Harpy, Smut, Woodranger,
Bristle, Chaser, Tempest, Blackcoat, Blanch, Shepherdess,
Killbuck, Surefoot, Glutton, Wolfet, Spot. May the Spartan
hounds destroy you. At last the deer head in all its reverie
elongating out into view, going up with the other glassy
eyes fixed on the wall, gazes moving on past Actaeon or
Ishtar or dialogue or language.

BIRD CARTOGRAPHERS

With names based in geography—
Amami woodcocks plan
from three hundred feet, wayfinding
a crepuscular scope high over
concise papyrus. Mountain
goldfinches outline early, before
the borders and boundaries have gone
to print, in undulating scale,
each dip punctuated by a
per-chik-o-ree. Baltimore orioles,
modelling reality, weave compass
roses that hang from branches.
California quail invent as many
as twenty toponyms at once. Forest
robins, giving short runs of chirrups,
tint layers and shade hills
to represent relief. South American
bitterns draw in reeds and cattails,
where they camouflage bias well,
considering purpose and audience,
as wingbeats select physical traits.
Australian pelicans work
together to design legends and then
scoop them up, conveying in lines
and broken V's as they chart
on flat media. Northern flickers
seek out the Robinson projection
rather than Mercator. Eastern
kingbirds flash a red pen
when eliminating irrelevant
features. Falcon-shaped, graceful and gray,
fledglings of Mississippi
kites reduce complexity and keep extra
drafting material for atlases.

Savannah sparrows gather ten times
their weight in detail to orchestrate
the ratio of land to water,
call a light *tsu*. Carolina
chickadees, cleaner edge of cheek patch,
mark dots of cities and dashes
of contours using a broad palette.
Inca doves huddle in labels
for accuracy, experimenting
in styles of fonts, forming
patterns up to four symbols long.
Often stained with ink, sandhill cranes
sketch by pumping their heads,
configuring the world in latitudes
and longitudes and wavy terrain,
a bugled chatter to create the key.
Flame-coloured western tanagers
chirr in the reflected gestalt of
aesthetically pleasing navigation.
Kentucky warblers sing the same
song about mapmaking their whole lives.

Two words in h&—Duke. Ellington.
Turn off the broadb&, cue up *Money Jungle*
& *The Far East Suite* & *Masterpieces*.

These wetl& whales are whales, I'm telling you.
In the cold & dark & remote, the epitome of style,
calls rivalling quicks&.

Crazy embellishments emerge from headst& chording,
ghost notes run up & down & beforeh&,
a polished balance between written & ad-libbed solos.

After the swing gl&, small pods & smaller combos,
the whole str& on the same melodic drift,
new harmonies that dem& the repertoire.

We're not talking about practice & a sweatb&.
Debut tunes playing off each other & trading counters.
A strident br& grabs the spotlight for several measures.

Yet another versatile line born in Greenl&,
growing up off the coast of Labrador & Finl&,
enough chops to start their own b& by age twenty.

Serenade the s& baleen—
a lot's happening on gr&st& tonight,
a who's who of contrab& & lapl& chorus.

Can you keep up? Exp& the tempo immediate.
Ampers& rhythms composing freeform codas,
improvised scales & keys & freeh& rising over the arctic top.

A little soli bending & stretching at will.
Wintering shorth& bebop, poise that lives up to the hype.
Each season a new take on wonderl&.

PHOTOGRAPHS OF BUILDINGS.
BY DIANE ARBUS

(I)

Chimneys can't push out but so much steam, even the outline's unfocused in blurry vapour. A quiet loosening of rigid matter. And how far they jut into the postsecular project of this guy, the sky. Just imagine such alternatives. Down lower squat the furnaces, lesser pipes blast about, the uptake, the downcomer, the day gang for the night gang. Beware the furrow of its brow. Sparks drip and stain, or stain and drip? The amorous coupling of iron to carbon, mouthpiece for the young. Revealing chiton flutters in the blower system's wind. Alloy in the right elements, manganese one of them. Multifaceted metal moves in narrow runnels, molten orange for sure, but the channel of cobalt blue.

(II)

From near the centre of the city, a glass veneer playing at crystalline mirage, tubular setbacks towering to a firmament lobby with overhanging eaves, down the elevator conundrum to the cluttered first floor of an American chain hotel. Signs of curtain walls and a steel underbelly, one still on offer. This whole scheme, the conglomerate's ruse to expand our sensorium, to force us to grow new organs. Talk about protest, pigeons pay the bill by chopping wood, sorting mail or refilling the icehouse. Lauding the Weather Underground, the weather under the ground. How much do the rooms remind you of home? The bell for the bellhop might ring with a new clapper. Silver ash panelling with plaster reliefs depicting the six seasons in India, a given.

(III)

Like the town collaborated and gave their best stolen
keepsakes for a final hub and resting place. Arrowheads
beside phonographs, cracked pottery beside shark teeth.
Dished out in pie slices by the atrium's serving knife
staircase. Part gift shop. A replica baseball to strike out Pete
Rose. Part catechism. Have you tried the Dutch stuff? Seen
the smuggled oolong tea? Checked out our barbed wire
collection? Inescapable pastiche of layer upon layer. Knick-
knacks chart the few highs—the full quiz and half answers
of a road trip, some middling kind of tranquility. The few
lows—that disorienting disaster, those corrupted mutations
in built space. Plexiglass displays catch all the children's
fingerprints, smudges from five hundred varieties of spun
candy and sweets.

Orpheus's first descent into hell
came when she sang about her own death
on local radio. She throated specks,
motes, planks and beams of shape-note singing.
Beyond the rivers Styx and Acheron,
each stride of string a crisp, articulate snap.
Twenty or so acoustic tunes led her
to where she could sing about a family
undivided, her blessed King James past,
her damned penchant for suffering, sing
about sirens in yellow jackets wearing
ten-gallon hats, about protecting
mosaics palimpsest. A truth-telling
spiritual guide suggested she expound
upon charisma, chimera, in go-go-
between mercy, with grace to boot.
But the invisible listeners,
tempest of jibes crowding around their
receiver dials, demanded her demise
every Wednesday at six p.m. sharp.
Light as a feather. Stiff as a board.
She had to cast off alternative endings,
her mishmash of allusion, and join them
in the tearing apart to nothing more
than an old car. Even after function
had been raked away to reveal caked-on oil,
faded paint, rusty drumlin of junk,
a profile remained, would remain remaining.

the still-dormant volcanoes of Japan ⊗ National Pi Day ⊗
have ⊗ hold ⊗ breathing and swallowing in unison ⊗
your health ⊗ peanut butter converted to diamonds ⊗ infinity ⊗
the abundance of shades of red ⊗ the have-beens ⊗ atoms ⊗
frozen air bubbles ⊗ gravity ⊗ duct tape wedding gowns ⊗
the fear of creepy dolls ⊗ fish that walk on soil ⊗ Adams ⊗
decomposing hot dogs ⊗ webworms on fungus-cocooned trees ⊗
the world's largest perennial flower ⊗ you ⊗ me ⊗ us ⊗
solar neutrinos ⊗ that waterfall in Hawaii that flows backwards ⊗
the fingerprints of koalas ⊗ ardour ⊗ potato batteries ⊗
the Colossus ⊗ eyes that dart eighty times a second ⊗ being well ⊗
Spoonerism Day ⊗ real flamingoes ⊗ a good stint ⊗
glittering shores ⊗ volcanic lightning ⊗ the are-nows ⊗
snails that sleep for decades ⊗ femurs ⊗ bliss ⊗ pink lakes ⊗
the Big Bang ⊗ crickets detecting music through their knees ⊗
crystal caves ⊗ the two-thousand-pound heart of a blue whale ⊗
beefalo ⊗ reusable water bottles ⊗ icebergs staying icebergs ⊗
the unknown colour of dinosaurs ⊗ barking sand dunes ⊗
cell service on Mount Everest ⊗ the maybes ⊗ well-being ⊗
cockroaches living underwater ⊗ reflective salt flats ⊗
garlic mustard seeds ⊗ Mother Goose Day ⊗ ligers ⊗
fringe-shaped coral reefs ⊗ magnetism ⊗ friendship (or not) ⊗
A.I. (or not) ⊗ hanging gardens ⊗ Byzantium ⊗ Rodin ⊗
every day lasting a second longer than the day before ⊗

WINGED DIVER AT THE LIMINAL

aka The Canadian Citizenship Ceremony, aka The CCC

Liquid faces ocean-worn, eyes deep-set
to take cover from the gale of our
metropolitan sea. Fellow newcomers.

Cracked fissures hold spray, while the tie that binds
moves fast to moor us together. Ample
time to wonder about data checkpoints,

about coarseness, who's woven courtliest.
When the wind drops, the *Diver* will head through
the polymorphic ceremony.

Great opener. Boundless leveller.
Et cetera, et cetera. Bow full
of prospects. Anthems sung.

When caught with the certificate,
commingle and retrofit. Pledges throw
their haul as far as they can past the swell.

Four walls shuffled up and dealt with drywall
and primer. Slabs of beached doors wallow,
melting and growing new skins with each oath.

Divided trees stretch horizontal.
Rocks shrink frostbitten. Winter has reached
the *Diver,* overturned and sheltering

untraceable roots or expat roles,
belonging just beneath, sojourned
twelve feet under in snow.

The planet Mars. One million years ago.
You see pyramid forms squatting in a sunken area.
Severe clouds moving in, more like a dust storm.
Towers of glassy surfaces and straight angles blown down.
Shadows of steeples, tall and thin.
Deep inside a canyon, sheer walls that go on forever,
huge sections of sleek stone. The gusts stride on overhead.
An obelisk at the end of a long avenue.
Ripped up and thrown like a javelin.

Now move degrees west.

You see a cluster of square shapes flush with the ground,
radiating patterns, reflecting electric light, the gist of it.
They etch channels, intersect aqueducts, carve roadbeds.

Now move degrees south.

A refuge from the gale. A chamber stripped of furnishings.
People hibernating in pale silk,
ancient citizens past their epoch.
They're preparing a group to find someplace new.
To escape their failing planet. Gearing up. Matt Damon's here.
You go with them on their journey.
All very cosmic, like kids' pictures of space.
Rockets with comet tails, globes with facial expressions.

Now move.

A place with volcanos and gas pockets.
A volatile plane, but with plants! Strange plants!
Never seen such green. Emerald green. Sage green.
Olive green. Pea green. Mint green. Fern green. Basil green.
Moss green. Lime green. Pear green. Pickle green.
Cactus green. Shamrock green. Pistachio green.
Seaweed green. Seafoam green. Frog green. Alligator green.
Crocodile green. Parakeet green. Juniper green. And pine.

We brought with us the rhyme royal ditches of *Tintamarre*,
back through the rectory,
planning a next next return to our deserted *maison*,
for a claiming back of roots and beach.

Nous sommes allés on that *de rigueur* pilgrimage to Forest Hill graveyard,
standing on the tombstone pillars there,
to attend to our choice of strong drink.

Reaching in bags full of apples,
our mentors would send forth beams of fruit,
on towards any unsuspecting heads,
warning us to watch *pour le signe* governed by atoms.

The work—
wrestling with *divers timbre*, where we continued on in lockstep,
weaving meat out of dry sinew,
a knot of syntax out of curly brackets.

Curtains might have opened with the rise of Mercury.

And on came "Orion,"
a first publication in *Patchwork Screen Magazine*,
quatre cents lines of wheeled hipbone and grindstoned nose,
plus the Fundy Coastal Drive.

To seek the hands of our partners,
we took jobs at *écoles*,
growing *barbes* and wearing *lunettes*.

We danced a *danse*,
dubbing ourselves the older hacks.

ON ANXIETY

Soon you'll sow seeds of demurral near the old dread.

Embrace lacuna from closet to arcade.

Against the million Bobbies across this land,

you need sanctuary, a holing-up.

Like you know you cannot withstand their force,

so why not let them run their course?

GHAZAL FOR HOPE

Were you or were you not on the floor because your hurt hip hurt so
      bad that's how I feel
and I feel like the pain is right there I'm in so much pain cutting right
      through my year

Exhausted when exhausting when you went to school in your Toyota
      out-of-sorts
car full of unwell soil the kids asked for shrubs with a timer set for
      Happy New Year

What are you trying to make quinoa salad or a random mashed potato
      dish rather buy
all the ingredients for chicken bone broth soup red pack blue packs to
      let you buy back years

Everything's so uncomfortable so I can't do anything I can do I can't
      really stand up
did you tell me that we're all ransacked well she's got the twinge
      shared twinge of so last year

I hope that I hope that they're back in good health because we heard
      nothing we just messaged
I'm going to message them about how they got better yeah yeah never
      in a million years.

What I mean and stuff like transferring like your hurt and stuff and
      relievers all transparent
I mean speaking happens online for the next doctor and Christmas
      comes but once a year

So when you think about ailing it's a first year plus a second I'm seeing
      a three-year program
with you a year am I a year in person yearly is a year and a bit of
      another golden year

The heart of being ill you just agree to trust multiple aches there so
      they'll be there
even if you only have one major problem now they're checking two
      problems a year

Residing in residence is not pleasant in agony so why don't you
    iMessage the Snapchat
you feel something's wrong I sent you some sore thing you get and I
    get the joke of the year

I think that you should call your friend he's like you are so you'll be
    friendly friends with him
and you're the same old people in young bodies so we're sure you're
    both okay with dog years

When you found the letters of your first name in your last name you
    knew then the discomfort
the riddle of anatomy the source of strain to find the ant in slant to find
    the ear in year.

A painting of

a mountain landscape;
a landscape with a river;
a landscape with trees and a body of water;
trees with yellow and red leaves;
a mountain range;
a forest with trees and a stream;
a river with red leaves;
a landscape with mountains and water;
a tree by the water;
a mountain range reflected in a lake;

trees and snow; trees and snow; trees and snow;

a snow-covered tree in a snowy forest;
a tree stump on a hill;
a landscape with rocks and trees;
a mountain surrounded by a forest;
a lake with trees and hills;
a tree on a beach;
a tree on the shore of a lake;

trees and water; trees and water; trees and water;

a mountain and two lakes;
a white tree with orange leaves;
a landscape with a blue sky and clouds;
a river flowing through a rocky area;
a mountain and one lake;
a mountain range with snow;
a lake in the middle of a rocky landscape;
a lake with a single yellow tree;

hills and clouds; hills and clouds; hills and clouds;

a waterfall next to another body of water;
a group of trees with orange leaves;
a mountain range in the water;
a forest on a lake;
a snowy landscape;
a river and trees;

Landscape = hills. Water.

FALLEN BETWEEN
THE WANDERING ROCKS

We lost another tree branch last night.
Front yard. Eastern pine. (From wind or heavy snow.)
In a parallel episode, I've turned back to clay,
the potter disappointed by her wobbly pot.

I allow room for accident;
I join in the sports banter; I map the salt of the earth;
I travel with chefs in brown Macintoshes
as they uncover exotic dishes along side streets.
All from the comfort of a chesterfield.

Our favourite games include:
Vagaries, Mental Gymnastics, The Underdog, Spillage.

You know, old man, I think that nirvana reshuffles
into many different shapes. Lozenges for one.
Wrestling Proteus, I've seen the divine
take on any form of water, beast, fire or morning.

Snippets of people go about their dog-walking lives during lunch hour.
(Five or fewer phlegmy coughs per trip.)

A balled-up piece of paper advertising
the coming of Elijah floats down the river.
The Liffey will always flow this way (northwesterly),
at this speed (moderately slow).

Reconsidering familiarity as the fulcrum.
As I record the exact chemical formula and date
of all capsules taken in yet another chasm.

THE ANNEX

No, this is not a poem about FLW,
his inherent plasticity of organic forms,
his open-air atrium of rotunda and
circulation core, the golden mean and complete
geometries and all that. Riding the elevator
to the top and then descending the nautilus spiral,
each cycle corkscrew a pavilion of galleries.
This is a poem about the annex to that
celebrated museum, the tank and flusher
of the world's most famous toilet bowl. All limestone grid.
All rectilinear foil recapturing the scalloped,
sloped perimeter. A touch of the artist
in four rows of offset slits. Call it backing vocals.
This is not a poem about Taliesin, the Welsh
magician and priest, about the family motto,
y gwir yn erbyn y byd ("take the quick ramp to exit").
Not about the daily paint job of egg-finish white,
walls slanting like art easels in an inverted
Mesopotamian ziggurat. This is about
restoring the dome of heaven, reglazing
the central lantern. Cleaning out space and opening
the clerestories between turns. Balcony views
revelling in the original façades
of the monitor building from both the outside-in
and the inside-out. Why not a roof sculpture terrace.
Double-high ceilings that expand right by right angle.
This isn't about genius or bumps or terrazzo,
but about the gilded age of refurbishment.
Something that's tasteful, discrete, logical.
A quiet, beige backdrop. Reframing our buoyant
energy and unalloyed tartan cheer.
The splendid overhaul allowing us to peruse
a few horizontal flats, to wade through tangents.

AT THE FIRST FIG CLUB

After Edna St. Vincent Millay

A hothouse earth, your
fertile climate no one can hold a candle
to. A special interest group burns
at the sight of your pearls, at
what you garner together, both
for barons of compression spring ends
and moguls of the same ilk. It
might not be wise to will
social ciphers and threats, not
wise to open the last
frontier episode. The
genesis, herald, harbinger of night
comes from beyond the grave. But
your prefab bits and borrowed pieces, ah,
how they profess viable endeavours to my
soul! Resistance vital for foes
who feed us our own touchstones. And
your paradigm of contours, oh
how it shines in 3D glasses! My
stasis caters to a few select friends.
Your all-encompassing glow, it
transcends gurus, sparks
utopia.

LILACS

2022 is the year of the lilac, according to the almanac.

So tonight let's walk the trail behind our house.

To the bushes growing in very great plenty and already divided.

Find an offshoot. Plant it in our side yard where its scent can flourish in the full sun.

Water and wait. We'll alternate scions with random grafts,

until its flowers appear at eye level, appearing just before summer comes into season,

blooms lasting only a couple weeks. The shrub's sweetness clinging in the air days after.

Heady. Cloying. Permeating the whole neighbourhood.

They can grow for over a century, outliving the homes they were planted around.

The nymph's disguise. Pan's first pipe.

Our wedding. Lilacs in each windowsill. Their long stems in vases at the altar.

Carefree oval clusters hanging from the garden arch.

The pale pinkish-bluish-violet colour, called firmament,

complementing the white roses, your Spanish lace mantilla.

In the basement of the church. What potted plants did we give away at the reception?

Talk of keeping them alive. Of keeping our love alive. How many of them are still alive?

At least one of them must still be alive.

SUBURBIA AND BEYOND

What a privilege to get in these our automobiles, parked at homes
on the right side of redlining tracks,
                    where we've maximized all public goods.

Then unravel a realm of street signs in our drive to work,
taking that loophole of arterials to dodge the endless strip sprawl.

At the end of the day,
                    from feet back to wheels touching the tarmac,
a return trip bridging gaps horn to horn.

Point C stands for any errands done,
            the weekend with a few cul-de-sac experiments thrown in.

This, our smog panorama.

                    Exhaust parallels abound in the anti-city.

Encased in a rocket without much thrust,
                    hurtling through the cosmos somewhat.

If we squint, we can just make out the crop circles and circuit boards,
dried hydrangeas that blow across a frozen golf course like tumbleweeds.

THE LAST AGES

Meghalayan

Muscle diminished, revealing arteries that shot out.
No belt or suspenders could keep our pants up,
a world too wide for our shrunken frames.
Then to form twilight by speaking it aloud,
voices returning to treble, whistles in the sound.
We used to have an abode of clouds with push-pins
piercing cumulo-, nimbo-, cirro-.
Remembering the billows of our tacks,
we set about removing them one by one.
Once all that remained were tiny perforations,
we found pleasure in the still pools of a lake.
(Somewhere below the divine a paradisal spring.)
In the sun beating down against our balding heads.
In casting out of line, the reeling back.

Anthropocene

It began with missing a button, an absent face.
We walked around all day with sideways pouches
in our flannel of uneven shirttails.
But when we discovered the leaves of our ancestors down,
and the inherent fish stock imperiled the autumn after that,
we knew what we had done would now require careful study.
(An imperative towards reversals.)
Our blades of grass shortened to abbreviated punches.
The chiming of our Trinity test rendered us translucent.
We gaped at the vivid knob-like mushroom
as it lent a cylinder of ponderous smoke and then gave out.
Seeing ourselves in the countenance that now came,
distant relatives who appeared at our bedside
and whom we tried but could not name.

IMMUNOCOMPROMISED

A few-years-wait for injected antibodies
> *A few-years-wait for our son.*

to stop the body from attacking the body.
Light shone from the top of a syringe,
> *Light shone from the top of the mount*

threading its way through plunger and barrel
to sketch the outline of a single bead
> *to sketch outlines between barren plants.*

bubbling from the bevelled lumen.
Stroll up to the purple highlighter,
> *Stroll up to the worn summit,*

marking a spot for numbing cream,
the scent of grapes overpowering.
> *the scent of pine and cedar overpowering.*

Just above the swelling knee joint,
a sprinkling of rash scrubbed by alcohol wipe.
> *A sprinkling of mist scrubbed by ozone.*

Needle outstretched to part   *the glinting aura.*

And in the thicket, a lone ram, caught by its horns.

We read the riveting backstory first, a chronicle of burgeoning discovery, new races and planetary systems unfurling towards a black hole's outer limit. Then twilight wars shattered the macrocosm. As if an ancient beast stirred from slumber in a dark cloud. We found ourselves at the object of the game: to reclaim the empire by gaining a total of ten victory points. Components spread out before us. Map hexes, plastic spaceships, species sheets, decks of cards and enough counters to cover the entire table. To set it up you must create a whole galaxy. The rules of play consisted of stages of strategy, action and status updates. We broke them down phase by phase. What do you want to be when you grow up? Explorer, diplomat, scientist, merchant, general, engineer, minister, doctor, accountant. Enterprise forms the heart of your turn, though you may choose to pass. To tactics: land on unknown planets to garner more resources. Or: energize networks in a campaign to harness political clout. The prestige sequence allows you to repair damages, refresh satellites, redistribute tokens. Other concepts presented on the intricacies of asteroid fields, nebulae, supernovas and wormholes. Guidelines for voting in the galactic council, advancing along a knowledge web, exchanging contracts for above-board trade. Bonus command. Speaker control. And of course the battle round, ship to ship combat, where you must declare your attacks, roll combat dice, remove casualties, announce retreats. By the designer notes on page forty-four, our eyes had stared at the blue-to-white suns for too long, Canopus, Procyon, motes floating in our vision. We packed the multitude of universes back in its box and put it on a shelf in the basement.

HALF A GRAPEFRUIT

I found a note in your jeans the other day
while doing laundry, creased and folded
to fit into your watch pocket. It said
in your most careful scrawl: *half a grapefruit.*
I stared at the yellow sticky note,
trying to glean its significance,
to imagine the moment you write it down,
how you look up and away and think:
yes, half a grapefruit.

What I need to...

What I want for...

Maybe the start of
a grocery list or the beginnings
of a balanced breakfast.

What I remember:

how my grandmother ate them. Halved along
the equator, sprinkled with sugar.
She had her own special spoon serrated
at the tip for digging out segment
by segment, then squeezed leftover
juice into a glass. Now, we peel and eat them
like oranges. Alice Munro has a story
with the same name. I picture you
walking in the woods, the audiobook
paused as some revelry of clarity
insists so strongly that you write it down,
slip in your pocket, forget to give to me.

THE EVIL STEPSISTERS

On their e-cigarette break, letting the diagnosis roast awhile
    with brooms and dustpans,
a one-hundred-degree heat index inside their silk
    and polyester costumes.
Both cite Hippocrates, grasp a gentle blow between the fourth
    and fifth expert opinions.
From behind a facade declaring *Cast Members Only,*
    Watch Your Step,
they're doing more work now—deep breath in, let the vanilla
    fill your lungs,
a slow exhale, vaping in clouds that rival the greatest volcanoes
    and chimneys—
than they do standing there, same self-mocking scowl
    plastered on their mugs.
Notions heliocentric: Why shouldn't they prance about? Butt in line?
    Ride the carousel?
Beads of sweat trickle down to meet their vape tanks. They wipe
    the lather as salty souvenirs
of all those who came before them. Take comfort in company.
    Symptoms of melancholy—
too much black bile the crux of lethargy and the lack
    of get-out-of-bed-free cards.
That little golden fairy that pleased Step-Stepfather with her report
    of mortal ailments—
palsy of the tongue, too active a wandering womb. Stepmother enters,
    lights a cigarette.
She recommends shaved heads, quilted caps soaked in perfumes
    to fume them over,
with herbs of a self-worth nature. A lavender salve completes
    the comprehensive regimen.
She plays the red embers against a feathered boa, imagining
    the perfect excuse—
spontaneous combustion sure is a problem this August.
    Alas, the spark breeds no flame.
Are real feathers not flammable?

ODE TO SLANG

You know and I know
and Baudelaire knows
the concept with the most slang—
I've counted phrases in the thousands.

The couples who might remember
the informal patter of the 1920s,
have great-grandchildren who go to shoptalks
for the experience of this cant and lingo,
living in a made-up word for a time,
testing the gap between standard and colloquial usage.

They'll come back home again,
only changed in the local vernacular.

(I)

Sprinkle the outbuildings around the main house. A wire mesh of cribs and coops. Carve a ring around each tree with a hatchet. Eight inches from the ground. To girdle them, to let them die slowly, acres of leafless telamons. Sunlight reaches the forest floor to lift up corn inflorescence. Slash to cash crops. Tobacco starved of nitrogen. And it takes five years or more before you can eat any apples. Mules still pull straight. Ignore the slips, glides, gullies, the rock-choked creek beds, sunken banks forming a cicatrix. You must replant the wheat to tassel; use the uncovered stones for a fence rebuild. Exhaustion cannot settle. Let the river. Invent your own measures to control pests, to mechanize the landscape. Cleave or cut your chains from the substratum. Ten feet of residuum gone. Gaze down at fatty marrow. Ponder a while on DDT versus birds versus malaria versus weeds. In the end, the loam will not give up on you until the entrance of seedless fruit.

(II)

Timber hems in towns until we push all the way to a panorama. Brush and sawdust form a new mini-forest on the flooring for the kids to crawl through. As foxfire glows. Haul the choicest hardwood to a nearby mill, fifty cents a ring. Build a splash dam to fill and then open the gate. Watch the flood, slick with firma in its widening path. Make Crystal Creek run muddy, bask in the misnomer. Saw a two-man crosscut until the roots let go. Lumber will course in an unbroken rill. Stir on a large scale the broad zone of sheared, metamorphosed limbs by number by hectare. What you'll love most, how the buzzing becomes almost lackadaisical. You no longer notice the chainsaw caper. Railroads open the way to clearcut. Steam loaders snake logs to flatbed cars. Trunk lines, secondary slides, spurring iron cobwebs. Pluck the woods pristine. Then pack up the boxcars amid the pledge of replanting.

(III)

Now we can peel back the thick mantle, see the insides. Does our old basement join in the folding of rocks? In burying sinew? Wriggle in horizontal or shimmy vertical, conclude a gaping maw, or drift along the stratum to tunnel flue patterns. It's your choice. The room-and-pillar move works in two-butt headings. Inaugurate an underground grid pattern, complete with ribbon-and-scissors ceremony; just don't speed through the yellow-lighted intersections. Down there, think of A. Think of B. The weight of ceiling between you and the past waxes sentimental. Don't listen to the crystalline. Who said trucks? Vise-like cold annihilates hands; still perceive them. Night-dark nothing like this sediment until the seams play out. Spot warblers coughing up a damp dust that covers everything. Inject an oxidant for in situ deposits. Where does the coal go? Who knows. Not here. Mine the mountain to mere outline.

(IV)

Arrive before the sun with your headlamp on, the procession like early morning fireflies all around the height. Great drab beetles straddle the slopes and kneel at stagnant pools; they sip runoff. Toss bread at the ducks or geese that wander the roads. Disrupt your habitat inside a cacophony of babble, an industrial racket. Block streams escorted by gob piles of tailings. Release cyanide into avant-garde chemistry. Disposal of thick slurry will take shape in a manmade pond, a sinkhole; reinforce the dam or let it meander to the ocean in an amorphous submarine. And what about safety props? Set them near a rich chimney vein. Utilize your element of surprise. Of trickery. Dig test pits to chart the geology and surrounding outcroppings. Prepare prefatory maps for each day's effort. Drive casing through the deep overburden to reach a solid base; raise and drop a seven-hundred-pound hammer, your tried-and-true pulley system, on the drill cathead. Now diesel. Now vermilion. Vibrate. Blast.

(V)

Think like a drone bee. Below the trill Whitman strain
sermonizes the funereal bass of what's deceased. No longer
need to pry loose from the marl. No longer earth. How
much is a rodent worth? How much money for this
wildflower? Cut the engine and listen. On Mars there's no
atmosphere of spring flycatchers, just basalt and brick
powder. In shallow-seated valleys, remove the word diverse
and its derivatives from your language. Rule the newly
paved routes with brakes in endless cavalcade. Tamp
ANFO explosives into a lattice of holes, then send sprays
of dirt a hundred feet up to linger. Reduce to rubble the
bowed tops. Until we engulf the remaining green-island
peaks in a sea of brown and raw and soot. Mold the terrain
in benches, a likeness of slope in wide concentric contours.
Ignore buffer zones and flatten the sine curve to zero.
Impoundments hold the sludge and may rupture through
old catacombs. Plan on it. Rehabilitate by smoothing off
plateaus. Cover with a veneer of clay, soil, vegetation—
fast-growing Chinese bush clover or black locust; these
layers may erode, so put up more fences; groundwater and
wildlife should climb the chain links.

(VI)

Narrow the view in your windshield. Forget acid rain, forget your next of kin, your emergency contact. The lunch-bucket argument will play over and over as something feral slides out of sight, not local but continental drifting. Divide the river flow. Inundate the land in electrical power. Reclaim gravity and call it symbiosis. Extend the sprawl beyond hillsides. Time the periodic mudslides, record. Smell the drying fish; gather any from the surface. Their company out of step with our era. Nuclear fission raised on climatology. Can you count to ninety-two? Electrons, I mean. Enrich, split. Half-heartedly inspect leaky valves, mutated smokestacks. Amid jumbles of boulders, the gypsum pond should wane serene; mind wet spots on the walls as cigarette ash spills. Collect and heap up the anti-alluvium; let it drain at a leisurely pace. Reaffirm the sun and wind and demand likewise. Sidle up to drought. Sweep out the riches as a lasting unease settles over what's left.

NOTES

"It Seemed That We Had Hardly Begun And We Were Already There" derives its name from a line in *My Life* by Lyn Hejinian.

"Coincidental" contains a line derived from an interview with Morrissey: "I chose to name the group [...] The Smiths because I thought that it was time that the ordinary folk of the world showed their faces."

"You Wear The Forest" is a poem in response to a hat made by Trish Hirschkorn.

"Mars Exploration: May 22, 1984" draws inspiration from a report of the same name released by the CIA in 2000.

"At The First Fig Club" is a broken golden shovel of Edna St. Vincent Millay's "First Fig."

"Suburbia and Beyond" is a gloss of Lewis Mumford's chapter of the same name from *The City in History.*

ACKNOWLEDGMENTS

Thanks to the editors of *Prairie Fire, Hamilton Arts & Letters, The London Reader, The Malahat Review, Contemporary Verse 2, The Miramichi Reader, The Fiddlehead, The Dalhousie Review,* and *The Ampersand Review,* who published earlier versions of these poems. Thanks also goes to Fredericton's Poems in Public, the *Profanity Fair Chapbook,* the *#MeltdownPoetryBlog, elm & ampersand* Poem-a-Day, *Poetry Spotlight Series #51, From My Window: Atlantic Poetry Chapbook, Poetry Weekend Reader '22, Dusie: The Tuesday Poem,* the Atlantic Vernacular Project, and the Amadeus Choir Choral Collaboration, where some of these poems also first appeared.

Thank you to the New Brunswick Arts Board and the Canada Council for the Arts for their support during the writing of these poems.

Thank you to readers of these poems at various stages of their creation: Lisa Russ Spaar, Ross Leckie, Sue Sinclair, Nick Thran, Rita Dove, Charles Wright, Debra Nystrom, Gregory Orr, Anne Compton, and Luke Hathaway.

Richard Vaughan, you are missed.

Thanks to Shane Neilson and Jeremy Luke Hill at Porcupine's Quill. Shane, you really saw what was sticking when I threw a whole bunch of stuff at the wall. Jeremy, you really got what this manuscript was about with your incredible cover design.

Thanks to my family growing up, my parents, brother and sister, my cousins, aunts, uncles, and grandparents, especially my two grandmothers—Helen Lester and Jean Gwathmey.

Thanks to Lily and the rest of our family together—James, Joshua, Tally, Winnie, and Robert. Still the best us.

ABOUT THE AUTHOR

Matthew Gwathmey lives in Fredericton, New Brunswick, on Wolastoqey Territory, with his partner Lily and their five children. He studied creative writing at the University of Virginia and recently completed his PhD at UNB. He has published three poetry collections: *Our Latest in Folktales* (Brick Books, 2019); *Tumbling for Amateurs* (Coach House Books, 2023); and *Family Band* (Porcupine's Quill, 2024).